Pteranodon

Written by Ron Wilson
Illustrated by Doreen Edwards

Library of Congress Cataloging in Publication Data

Wilson, Ron, 1941-
  Pteranodon.

  (The New dinosaur library)
  Summary: Introduces the pteranodon, a kind of pterodactyl, or flying reptile, that lived on the earth during the age of dinosaurs.
    1. Pteranodon—Juvenile literature.   [1. Pteranodon.
2. Pterodactyls.   3. Prehistoric animals]   I. Title.
II. Series.
QE862.P7W55   1984   567.9'7   84-6839
ISBN 0-86592-201-2

Rourke Enterprises, Inc.
Vero Beach, FL 32964

Diplodocus

Pteranodon

Woolly Mammoth

Pteranodon

Allosaurus

Hypsilophodon

Ichthyosaurus

It was still dark when the old Pteranodon woke up. The younger Pterosaurs would have little to do with him. He was old and he didn't have as much energy as they did. He'd been out with them a few days earlier when they had stopped him from feeding at the old cove. They had made so much fuss that Pteranodon had gone off on his own. He had flown many miles and had found another bay.

It was a secret place and no Pterosaurs fed there. He had perched high above this new bay. Down below he could see the still clear waters spread out before him. Although it was deserted it was the sort of place which should have plenty of fish. Pteranodon didn't have time to search. Already it was beginning to get dark. He had to return to his nightly roosting place.

So today was a special day. He was going to leave. If he didn't do it soon other Pterosaurs were bound to find the place. Of course his old body would soon be too fragile to carry him. It was the first chance he had had to set off on his own. He wanted to go to the new cove just for peace and quiet. It seemed an ideal place with enough food for the taking. Yet no other Pterosaurs fed there. He wondered why.

The cliffs were still very quiet. Around him the sky was a beautiful pink. The sun would soon be rising. All the other Pterosaurs were still asleep. There was no sound. This was just the time for Pteranodon to leave. Before he moved Pteranodon had to be sure that no other creature was awake. He moved carefully. He was not careful enough. He disturbed a piece of rock which went crashing to the beach below. It was so loud that it would be a miracle if the other Pterosaurs were not awakened.

Pteranodon watched and listened. Below him he saw the form of another Pteranodon. He knew that if he disturbed it it would warn all the other Pterosaurs. Then the whole cliffs would be awake, and they would attack him.

He watched the creature carefully. It did not move. The sound had gone unnoticed by the sleeping animals. Pteranodon looked up above his head between the rocky cliffs. He could see the sky. He had enough room to launch himself without crashing into anything. He took off carefully from his resting place. His old limbs lifted him slowly above the cliffs. He managed to get away without making a sound.

He circled slowly before he headed south. The old Pteranodon had flown the route to his feeding ground many many times. He could probably have gotten there blindfolded.

He flew slowly, his aging wings would not carry him as fast as when he was younger. It was still early and he must fly on before he took a rest. He got into the strongest air currents.

He drifted inland not far from the coast. He was
sure there were a lot of enemies below. He had seen
many Tyrannosaurus on his other journeys. He flew
well above the tops of the trees. He was heading for his
usual feeding place. From high up he could see the long
shadows creeping over the countryside, as the sun came
up. He caught sight of many stirring dinosaurs below
him.

Doreen Edmond

Once he made it to the old cove he would find it easier getting to the new bay. A short way in front of him was a well known landmark. There was a small clump of trees which was used by some of the Pterosaurs as a resting place.

Pteranodon had travelled a long way. Every wing beat was more difficult. He felt very weary and he made his way to the group of trees. He flew around looking down to see whether any other creatures were there. He could not see any other signs of life. Pteranodon landed so that he could rest for a while. Soon something inside him told him he had to move. It wouldn't be long before the sun was fully up and every creature would be awake.

He felt better after a few minutes rest.
Pteranodon set off again, the air currents carrying him
much faster. Some distance in front was an outcrop of
rock. It roughly marked the halfway point of his flight
to his usual feeding place.

The old Pteranodon knew that there were very few resting places ahead, except for the jagged rock. He knew he must get there. Pteranodon passed over several clearings in the forest. He had time to look down. Already he could see signs of life. He saw an Euoplocephalus stirring. He heard a Tyrannosaurus bellowing. Soon the many sounds of the forest dwellers reached his ears. He was hungry so he had to keep going. He always knew he had to avoid danger.

Pteranodon would soon have to stop before the sun made it too hot for him to continue. If he didn't stop he would be seen. The rock was close. Pteranodon made for it. He circled it a few times before deciding it was safe to land. He grabbed it with his claws and soon settled down.

He had not eaten for a couple of days and he was very hungry. He had to stay here until tomorrow. Other Pterosaurs flew overhead. He looked up but he didn't recognize any from his particular flock.

Pteranodon looked down. He watched as a Triceratops fed on the fronds of one of the giant plants. The creature's body was large. It needed a great deal of food to satisfy its hunger. Soon it had stripped all the fronds from several plants.

In the distance another Triceratops fought savagely with one of its own kind. The old Pteranodon could hear the angry noises. He was very weary. The sounds became fainter. Soon he was asleep. He woke many hours later. The sun had set and everywhere was quiet and dark except for the light from a full moon.

Pteranodon knew he had to set off again. He cleared the rock without a sound except for the flapping of his leathery wings. Shortly he recognized the waters of his usual feeding place below him. He needed to find the new bay.

He soared higher, using the air currents. Soon he had a much better view of the ground below him. He circled for a few minutes and then went off in an easterly direction. He flew on until he saw a glint of silver below him. It was the moonlight shining on the waters of the new bay.

Pteranodon flew high above the bay to see what it was like. He could not see clearly and he flew lower. There were many jagged rocks around the edge of the water. He had to fly carefully so that he didn't fly into them.

There was no sign of life. All the other creatures must be resting. Pteranodon landed on a rock overhanging the water. He settled down to wait for the coming day. Within a short time he was asleep.

When he awoke the sun was shining brightly. Pteranodon looked around him. He could not see anything. Nothing stirred on the rocks. Nothing moved in the grass. The waters of the bay were clear. Pteranodon could not see any fish. So this was why the other Pterosaurs had never been here to feed. There was nothing to eat. Pteranodon looked around him. He flew down for a closer look.

The Pterosaur had not eaten for two days now. He had flown a long way. He looked around for something to eat. He searched the bay but there was nothing. He needed food. The only place he knew was the old cove. He would have to go there and mix with the other Pterosaurs. He hoped they would not have noticed that he had been missing.

Pteranodon set off, the sun's position telling him which way to fly. The wide area of water of the old cove came into view. He could see the other Pterosaurs and he slowed down. He must fly in low so that he wouldn't be seen. Pteranodon did this and landed safely on a rocky ledge. He watched until the other Pterosaurs dived down to catch their food. Then he joined them. There was plenty of fish and he ate a lot. He kept his eye on the other Pterosaurs. They didn't seem to notice him.

He ate as much as he could and returned to a rock to digest. Soon it was time for the Pterosaurs to return to their nightly roosting sites. Pteranodon went with them. He flew a little way behind the rest of the group as he always did.

He arrived back a few minutes after the other Pterosaurs. He needed somewhere to rest. All the rocky ledges were full. He flew low over the tops of the cliffs. The other resting Pterosaurs attacked him. At last he found a vacant ledge some way from the other creatures. He landed gently and within minutes he had settled down and was asleep.

Interesting facts about . . .
Pteranodon

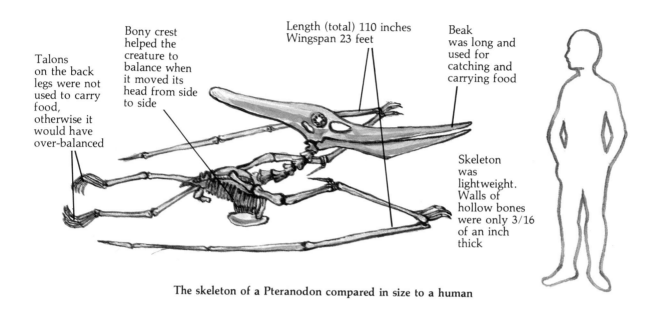

Talons on the back legs were not used to carry food, otherwise it would have over-balanced

Bony crest helped the creature to balance when it moved its head from side to side

Length (total) 110 inches
Wingspan 23 feet

Beak was long and used for catching and carrying food

Skeleton was lightweight. Walls of hollow bones were only 3/16 of an inch thick

The skeleton of a Pteranodon compared in size to a human

The Age of Dinosaurs

Although dinosaurs dominated the earth during the "Age of Dinosaurs", there were other creatures as well. Pterosaurs, which included Pteranodon and Pterodactylus, were among these. As the large dinosaurs roamed the land, large creatures were also flying overhead.

When did Pteranodon live?

Scientists divide the life of the earth into eras. Pteranodon lived during the Mesozoic Era which started 225 million years ago and ended about 65 million years ago. Each era is divided into periods. In the Mesozoic Era there were three periods. These are called Triassic, Jurassic and Cretaceous. The Triassic was the first and the Cretaceous the last. Pteranodon lived during the Cretaceous Period.

What was Pteranodon?

Pteranodon wasn't a dinosaur. It was a Pterosaur. Pterosaurs developed from reptiles. They were able to fly. If we look at Archosaurs like Podopteryx we can see similar features between these and Pterosaurs. Normally, when we think of reptiles we think of snakes and lizards. Pterosaurs are different. They developed wings and could fly.

Pteranodon was one of the Pterodactyls. The oldest known Pterosaur is one called Eudimorphodon. This creature lived in Italy during the Triassic period. The smallest Pterosaur was Pterodactylus. It was about the size of a sparrow. Pteranodon was thought to be the largest Pterosaur. Recently, a bigger Pterosaur called Quetzalcoatlus was discovered in Texas.

What size was Pteranodon?

Pteranodon was a large creature. It had a wing span of about 23 feet. This is twice the wing span of the albatross which is the largest bird living today. From the place where the wing joined the body to its tip it measured 4 feet. The *total* wing span of an albatross is no more than 11 feet.

How did Pteranodon fly?

Scientists have been fascinated by Pteranodon. They have made models of the Pterosaur. They have tested these in wind tunnels. Pteranodon had leathery wings. The tests in the wind tunnels showed that it could fly well. When it flew over the oceans it used air currents. These often carried it a long way. Pteranodon would have spent much of its life gliding on these currents.

However, if it managed in the air, Pteranodon had problems on the ground. Tests showed that it would have found it difficult to take off from flat surfaces. Scientists are not sure what happened when the creature landed on the ground. When it had a place from which to launch itself, it could use the air currents to help it get into the air. There are many of these currents around cliffs and over the oceans. Birds living here today still use the same method. It means they don't have to use as much energy.

Scientists were puzzled by a strange crest which Pteranodon had on its head. At first it seemed that it added a lot of weight. This would make flying even more difficult. In fact, it only weighed about 6 oz. because it was made of thin bone. Tests showed that the crest helped Pteranodon to balance when it moved its neck. If the crest hadn't been there it would have needed large muscles. These would have made it even heavier.

What did Pteranodon feed on?

Pteranodon fed on fish. It had a long beak. It also had claws on its back legs. It didn't use these when fishing. If it had carried fish in these claws it would probably have overbalanced. The claws were used for hanging onto cliffs and ledges. When Pteranodon wanted to feed it could glide from the cliffs and pick up food. It could also land on water. When it was flying over the oceans it dived into the water to catch its food.

What were Pteranodon's bones like?

We have said that Pteranodon was large. Apart from its enormous wing span, its body measured 9 feet long. Scientists were surprised when they looked at the creature's bones. They were very thin. It was strange that the creatures managed to dive into the sea without breaking its bones. With light bones, Pteranodon found it easy to launch itself. It probably only weighed about 40 pounds, which was very light for its size.

Things to do

Pteranodon spent much time gliding around when in the air. Can you find the names of some living animals which use gliding to get them from place to place?

Can you find out how large birds like the albatross manage to use their wings for gliding over the oceans?

We don't know exactly what Pteranodon looked like. People who have studied the creature have managed to get an idea. See if you can make a model Pteranodon.

Scientists found that Pteranodon's light wings made it fly easier. See if you can make gliders with light and heavier material. Which glides best?

Make cut outs of some of the animals in the book. Color them — make sure they are to scale. Then stick them on a large sheet of paper. Cut out plants and add these. Color the rocks and the sea. This will give you your own picture of what it was like when Pteranodon lived.

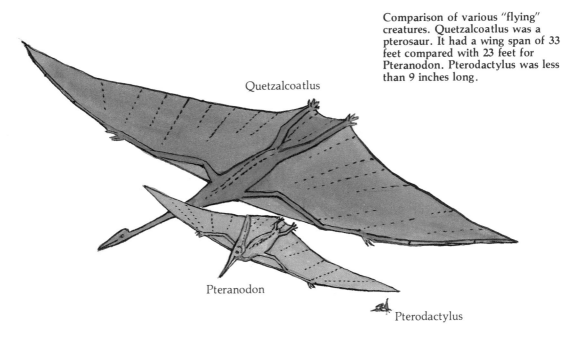

Comparison of various "flying" creatures. Quetzalcoatlus was a pterosaur. It had a wing span of 33 feet compared with 23 feet for Pteranodon. Pterodactylus was less than 9 inches long.

Quetzalcoatlus

Pteranodon

Pterodactylus

Sylvia G. Margolin,
lovingly remembered

First edition

Library of Congress Catalog Card No. 88-80666.

10   9   8   7   6   5   4   3   2   1

Published simultaneously in Canada
by Little, Brown & Company (Canada) Limited

Printed in Singapore for Harriet Ziefert, Inc.

Good Night, Everyone!

HARRIET ZIEFERT
ILLUSTRATED BY
ANDREA BARUFFI

LITTLE, BROWN AND COMPANY
BOSTON   TORONTO

It had been a busy day.
Harry was tired and wanted to go right
to sleep. He collected his toys and said,
"Good night, everyone. It's time for bed."

Harry put his bear on his chair.
"No nonsense, bear," he said.
"Now go to sleep."

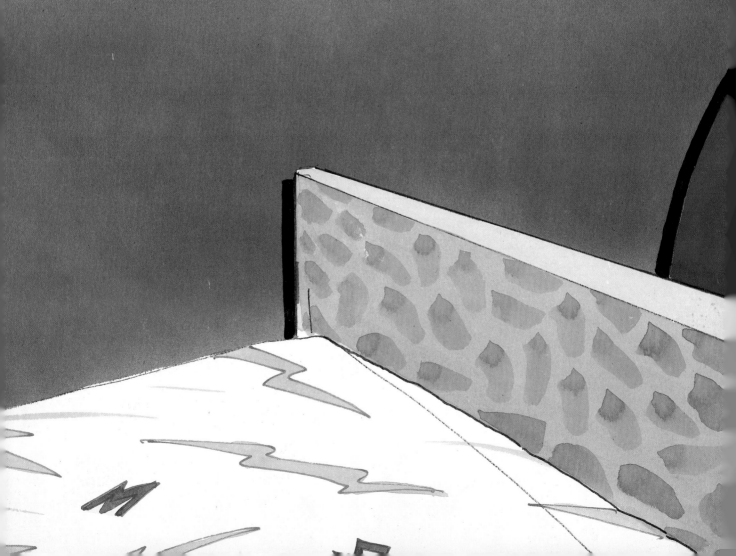

Harry put his monkey near his bed.

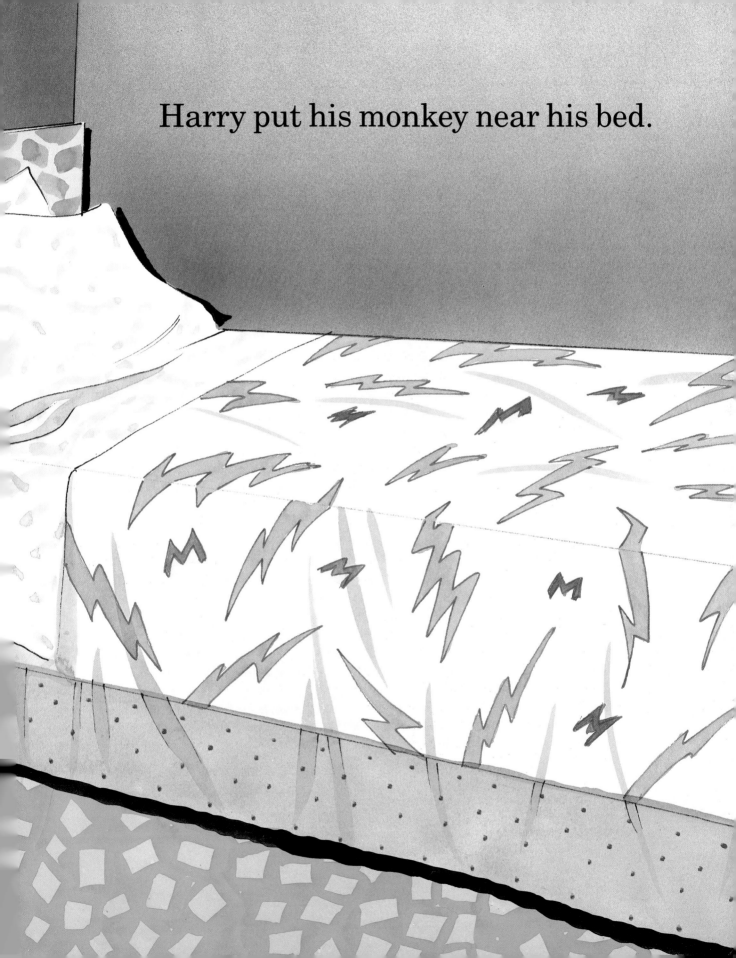

He put his mouse near his slippers.

He put his lamb near his pillow.

Harry climbed into bed,
turned off the lamp, and
everybody went to sleep.

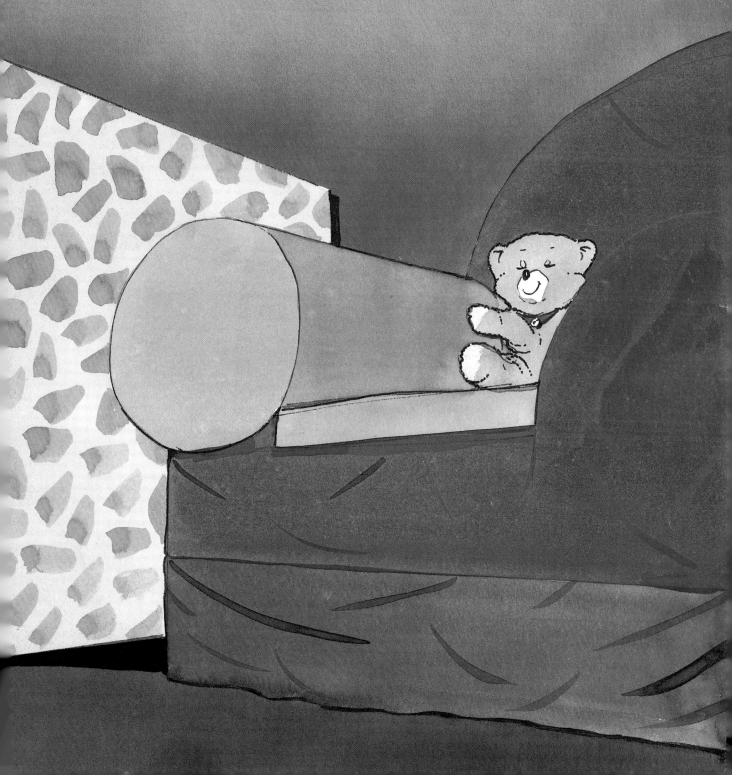

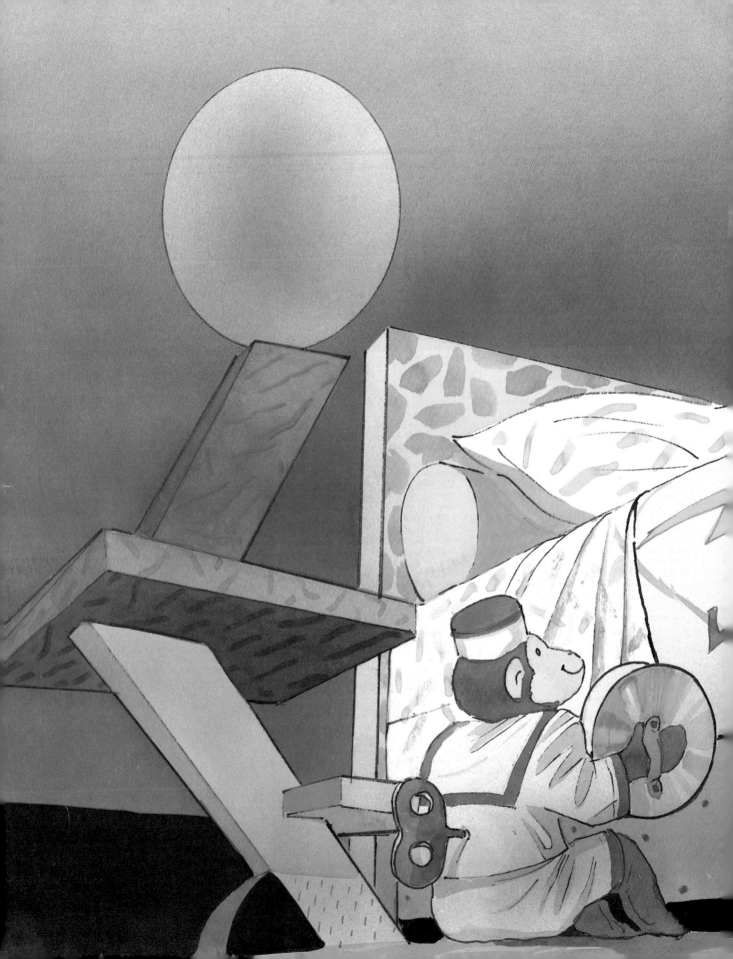

But not the lamb!
The lamb woke the monkey.
"Let's play," he whispered.

The monkey woke the bear.

The bear woke the mouse.

The mouse squeaked.
The lamb bleated.
The bear grunted.

The monkey said,
"Wind me! Wind me!
Wind me up!"

Harry woke up. "Be quiet!" he yelled.
"Didn't you hear what I said? Tonight
I'm *really* tired and I want to sleep."

But no one listened.
Not even the mouse.

So Harry hid the monkey under the bed

and he hid the bear under the chair.

He stuffed the mouse
into the slippers.

He shoved the lamb
under the pillow.

Then Harry climbed back into bed, turned off the lamp, and this time everybody went to sleep.

Good night, everyone!